MW00946900

RICHARD LUNDY

CAPPADOCIA TRAVEL GUIDE 2024-2025

Exploring the Must-See Attractions, Accommodations and Itineraries

Copyright © 2024 by Richard Lundy

All rights reserved. No part of this publication may be reproduced, stored or transmitted in any form or by any means, electronic, mechanical, photocopying, recording, scanning, or otherwise without written permission from the publisher. It is illegal to copy this book, post it to a website, or distribute it by any other means without permission.

Richard Lundy asserts the moral right to be identified as the author of this work.

First edition

This book was professionally typeset on Reedsy.
Find out more at reedsy.com

Contents

Introduction

About The Guide

Welcome to the ultimate guide for creating an unforgettable adventure in Cappadocia, Turkey. This comprehensive travel guide is your go-to resource, designed to help you navigate the stunning landscapes, rich culture, and hidden treasures of this remarkable region.

Inside, you'll find meticulously curated information to ensure a smooth and enriching experience. Whether you're a seasoned traveller or on your first journey, this guide caters to all levels of experience.

Here's what you can expect:

1. **Effortless Planning**: We'll provide you with all the knowledge you need to plan your trip seamlessly. From the best times to visit based on weather and personal preferences to visa requirements and essential packing tips, we have you covered.

2. **Must-See Attractions**: Embark on a fascinating journey through Cappadocia's iconic landmarks. Visit the awe-inspiring Göreme Open-Air Museum, admire the whimsical Fairy Chimneys, and enjoy a hot air balloon ride over the stunning landscapes. Explore mysterious underground cities and discover the peaceful beauty of hidden valleys.

3. Cultural Immersion: Go beyond the typical tourist spots and immerse yourself in Cappadocia's vibrant culture. We'll introduce you to the region's delicious cuisine, highlighting must-try local dishes that will leave you wanting more.

4. Perfect Accommodation: Find a variety of accommodation options to fit your budget and style. Whether you're looking for luxurious comfort in a hotel or resort, the social vibe of a hostel, or the charm of a local guesthouse, this guide will help you find the perfect place to relax after a day of exploration.

5. Itinerary Crafting: Let us help you plan the perfect Cappadocian adventure. We offer various meticulously planned itineraries, including a 7-day general itinerary, a 7-day culinary journey, and a romantic 7-day itinerary for couples.

6. Practical Essentials: Ensure a hassle-free experience with our comprehensive section on practical information. We'll provide details on currency exchange, transportation options, overcoming language barriers, and essential health and safety tips.

This guide is more than just facts and figures; it's your gateway to the magic of Cappadocia. By diving into its rich history, stunning landscapes, and vibrant culture, you'll create memories that will last a lifetime.

So, pack your bags, unleash your wanderlust, and get ready for an unforgettable journey to the heart of Turkey with this indispensable Cappadocia Travel Guide as your trusted companion.

* * *

History and Background

Cappadocia's mesmerising landscape is not just a visual delight; it's a testament to a rich and intricate history. To truly grasp the wonders of this region, a dive into its past is crucial. Prepare for a fascinating journey through time.

Millions of years ago, volcanic eruptions from Mount Erciyes, Mount Hasan, and Mount Güllü covered the region with ash and lava. Over time, relentless winds and rain carved these volcanic deposits into the surreal rock formations we see today, including the iconic Fairy Chimneys.

Early Civilizations Leave Their Mark

Human presence in Cappadocia dates back to the Palaeolithic era. The Hittites, a powerful civilization around 1600 BC, established their presence here, carving impressive rock sanctuaries and temples, some of which still stand today.

Kingdoms Rise and Fall

After the Hittite Empire's decline, Cappadocia saw the rise and fall of various kingdoms, including the Persians, Greeks, and Romans. Each civilization influenced the region's architecture, art, and religious practices.

Christianity Finds Refuge

With the rise of Christianity in the Roman Empire, Cappadocia became a refuge for persecuted Christians. They carved elaborate cave churches and monasteries into the soft volcanic rock, creating a lasting testament to their faith. The Göreme Open-Air Museum is a magnificent example of this era.

The Rise of Underground Cities

To protect themselves from constant invasions, Cappadocians engineered vast underground cities. These intricate networks of tunnels and chambers served as hidden sanctuaries during times of war. Derinkuyu and Kaymakli are two of the best-preserved underground cities, offering a glimpse into this fascinating chapter of Cappadocia's history.

Seljuk Turks and Beyond

The arrival of the Seljuk Turks in the 11th century marked a cultural shift in Cappadocia. While Christian influence diminished, Islamic art and architecture began to thrive. The region continued to be a cultural crossroads, influenced by Byzantine Greeks and Ottomans.

Today, Cappadocia is a vibrant region celebrating its rich and diverse heritage. Visitors can explore remnants of ancient civilizations, marvel at stunning natural landscapes, and experience the warmth and hospitality of the Turkish people. Understanding Cappadocia's history deepens your appreciation of the region, transforming your trip into a captivating exploration of a land where time seems to stand still.

Chapter 1: Planning Your Trip to Cappadocia

Best Time to Visit

Cappadocia's allure is ever-present, but the best time to visit depends on your preferences for weather, crowds, and activities. Here's a breakdown of the advantages and disadvantages of each season to help you decide.

Spring (April - June)
  Pros

- Pleasant weather with warm days and cool nights, perfect for outdoor activities like hiking and hot air ballooning.
- Fewer crowds compared to peak summer.
- Vibrant wildflowers decorate the landscape.

Cons

- Early spring (April) can be windy, potentially affecting hot air balloon rides.

· Prices start to rise as the tourist season begins.

Summer (July - August)
Pros

· Hot and sunny weather, ideal for enjoying pools or relaxing at cave hotels with terraces.
· Peak season for hot air ballooning with clear skies and calm winds.

Cons

· The hottest months can be uncomfortable, especially during midday.
· The largest crowds and highest prices of the year.
· Accommodation can book up quickly, so plan well in advance.

Autumn (September - November)
Pros

· Comfortable temperatures with warm days and cool evenings, great for sightseeing and outdoor activities.
· Fewer crowds compared to summer.
· Possibility of witnessing the grape harvest in some areas.

Cons

· Days become shorter as autumn progresses, reducing daylight hours.
· Some outdoor activities may have limited hours or be unavailable by November.

Winter (December - March)
  Pros

- · The quietest and most affordable time to visit.
- · Snow-dusted landscapes offer a dramatic and unique perspective.
- · Lower hotel rates and fewer crowds at popular attractions.

Cons

- · Colder temperatures and potential snowfall can limit outdoor activities.
- · Some restaurants and shops may have limited hours or be closed.
- · Hot air balloon rides may be less frequent due to weather conditions.

Additional Considerations

1. Festivals and Events: Cappadocia hosts several festivals throughout the year, such as the Cappadox Festival in May, featuring contemporary art and cultural events. If a specific event interests you, plan your trip accordingly.

2. Prices: Accommodation and activity prices fluctuate with the seasons. Shoulder seasons (spring and autumn) often provide the best balance between affordability and pleasant weather.

3. Personal Preferences: Consider what you enjoy most, warm weather for outdoor activities, cooler temperatures for sightseeing, a bustling atmosphere, or a quieter experience.

By weighing these factors, you can choose the perfect time to visit Cappadocia and ensure an unforgettable travel experience.

* * *

Geography and Climate

Cappadocia's appeal extends beyond its rich history and culture, featuring a captivating geography and unique climate that have shaped its landscapes and influenced its inhabitants for millennia. Located in eastern Anatolia, Cappadocia sits on a high plateau with an average elevation over 1,000 metres (3,280 feet) above sea level. This elevation contributes to its distinct climate. Volcanic activity millions of years ago shaped the dramatic landscapes seen today. Mount Erciyes, the region's highest peak at 3,916 metres (12,848 feet), stands as a majestic reminder of this fiery past. Ancient eruptions covered the region in ash and lava, forming the foundation for Cappadocia's iconic rock formations.

Over time, relentless wind and water erosion sculpted the volcanic deposits into a landscape of dramatic formations. The soft volcanic rock eroded unevenly, creating the famous Fairy Chimneys towering, cone-shaped structures capped with harder volcanic rock. These otherworldly pillars, along with valleys, mesas, and canyons, contribute to Cappadocia's breathtaking and ever-changing scenery.

Cappadocia's inland location and high altitude give it a continental climate with distinct seasons:

1. Hot and Dry Summers: Summers are typically hot and dry, with average temperatures reaching the mid-30s degrees Celsius (around 95 degrees Fahrenheit). Sunshine is abundant, making it an ideal time for outdoor activities like hot air balloon rides and exploring the valleys. However, be prepared for strong sun and pack accordingly.

2. Cold and Snowy Winters: Winters are cold, with temperatures dropping below freezing and frequent snowfall. The landscape transforms into a winter wonderland, offering a unique perspective for those who enjoy colder weather. However, some attractions and tours may have limited availability during this time.

3. Pleasant Spring and Autumn: Spring and autumn provide mild temperatures, making them ideal shoulder seasons for exploring Cappadocia. The crowds are typically smaller, and you can enjoy the region's beauty without the intense summer heat.

Sparse Rainfall and a Semi-Arid Environment

Rainfall in Cappadocia is scarce throughout the year, classifying it as a semi-arid region. The Taurus Mountains to the south block moisture from the Mediterranean Sea, contributing to hot, dry summers and ensuring clear skies and ample sunshine for most of the year.

Understanding Cappadocia's geography and climate will help you choose the best time to visit for your desired experiences. Whether you seek the warmth of summer or the tranquillity of winter, Cappadocia offers a captivating landscape waiting to be explored.

* * *

Visa and Entry Requirements

Before setting off on your unforgettable adventure to Cappadocia, it's essential to familiarise yourself with Turkey's visa and entry requirements. This guide will help you navigate the process smoothly, ensuring a hassle-free arrival.

Do You Need a Visa?

Many nationalities can visit Cappadocia, Turkey, for tourism purposes without obtaining a visa in advance. Here's a breakdown of the visa requirements:

1. Visa-Free Entry: Citizens of many countries, including most European nations, the United States, Canada, Australia, and New Zealand, can enter Turkey visa-free for stays up to 90 days within any 180-day period.

2. Double-check: Always verify the latest visa requirements with the Turkish Ministry of Foreign Affairs or your nearest Turkish embassy or consulate before your trip. Nationalities not mentioned above or those planning longer stays will likely require a visa.

E-Visa Option

For some nationalities, obtaining an electronic visa (e-Visa) online is a convenient option. This streamlined process allows you to apply for and receive your visa electronically before departure.

General Entry Requirements

Even if you qualify for visa-free entry, make sure you meet the following general requirements for a smooth immigration process:

1. Valid Passport: Your passport must be valid for at least six months beyond your intended departure date from Turkey and have sufficient blank pages for entry and exit stamps.

2. Onward or Return Ticket: Immigration officials may ask for proof of onward or return travel tickets demonstrating your exit from Turkey.

3. Sufficient Funds: While not always mandatory, it's advisable to carry proof of sufficient funds for your stay. This could be cash, credit cards, or travel documents demonstrating prepaid accommodation and expenses.

Staying Longer?

If you plan to extend your stay beyond the visa-free period or need a visa for longer stays or specific purposes like work or study, you must obtain a visa from a Turkish embassy or consulate in your home country before your trip.

Important Tips

1. Stay Updated: Visa requirements can change, so it's vital to check for the latest information from official sources well in advance of your trip.

2. Preparation: With a little planning and preparation, you'll be ready to bypass immigration smoothly and start exploring the wonders of Cappadocia.

By following these guidelines, you can ensure a smooth entry into Turkey and focus on enjoying your adventure in Cappadocia.

Packing Essentials

Ensuring you pack the right clothes and essentials will significantly enhance your Cappadocian experience. Here's a comprehensive guide to packing for this unique destination.

Considering the Climate

Cappadocia experiences significant temperature variations throughout the year. Summers are generally hot and dry, with average highs reaching the mid-80s Fahrenheit (around 30 degrees Celsius). Winters can be quite cold, with occasional snowfall, and average lows dipping below freezing (around 0 degrees Celsius). Spring and autumn offer pleasant weather, with comfortable daytime temperatures and cooler evenings.

Dressing in Layers

Due to the fluctuating temperatures, layering is crucial. Pack breathable, lightweight clothing for exploring during the day, such as t-shirts, shorts, or lightweight pants. Even in summer, evenings can get chilly, so pack a light sweater or jacket. For winter adventures, pack thermals, a warm jacket, gloves, a scarf, and a hat.

Footwear for Exploring

Comfortable walking shoes are essential for navigating Cappadocia's uneven terrain. Hiking boots are recommended if you plan on tackling challenging hikes. For exploring towns and villages, sandals or comfortable sneakers are a good option.

Sun Protection

Cappadocia receives ample sunshine year-round, so pack a hat with a wide brim, sunglasses with UV protection, and sunscreen with a high SPF (30 or higher). Consider bringing a sun hat that can be secured with a chin strap for windy days on hikes.

Respecting Local Customs

When visiting religious sites like mosques or cave churches, it's important to dress modestly. Pack long pants or skirts that cover your knees and shirts that cover your shoulders. A scarf is a versatile accessory that can be used to cover your head or shoulders when needed.

Additional Essentials

Here are some additional items to consider packing for your Cappadocian adventure:

1. Reusable water bottle: Staying hydrated is important, especially during hot weather.
2. Swimsuit: If your hotel has a pool or you plan on visiting hot springs, pack a swimsuit.

3. Quick-drying towel: Handy for drying off after swimming or taking a hot air balloon ride.
4. Camera and accessories: Capture the magic of Cappadocia with a good camera and extra batteries.
5. Universal adapter: If you're travelling from outside of Turkey, pack a universal adapter to ensure you can charge your electronic devices.
6. Personal toiletries: Pack your usual toiletries, but remember that most hotels will provide basic amenities like shampoo and soap.
7. First-aid kit: Pack a small first-aid kit with essential medications like pain relievers, allergy medication, and band-aids.
8. Entertainment: Pack a book, journal, or download some movies/shows for entertainment during downtime or long journeys.

Remember

1. Check the weather forecast: Check the specific weather forecast for your travel dates before finalising your packing list.

2. Airline restrictions: Airlines may have luggage weight restrictions, so be sure to weigh your bags before departure.

3. Laundry: Consider doing laundry during your stay if you're packing light.

By packing strategically, you'll be prepared for anything Cappadocia throws your way, allowing you to focus on creating unforgettable memories.

Chapter 2: Must-See Attractions

Göreme Open-Air Museum

Among the surreal rock formations of Göreme Valley, the Göreme Open-Air Museum is a UNESCO World Heritage Site and the highlight of Cappadocia. This extensive complex features a mesmerising array of cave churches, monasteries, and dwellings carved into the soft volcanic rock, offering visitors a glimpse into the historical and artistic brilliance of past civilizations.

During the rise of Christianity in the Roman Empire, Cappadocia became a refuge for persecuted Christians. They ingeniously used the region's unique geological features to carve out a network of churches, monasteries, and living quarters from the soft volcanic rock. The Göreme Open-Air Museum represents the zenith of this monastic activity, with numerous churches and chapels dating from the 4th to the 13th centuries AD.

Apart from its architectural wonders, the Göreme Open-Air Museum is celebrated for its stunning Byzantine frescoes. These vibrant murals, adorning the walls and ceilings of the cave churches, depict scenes from the Bible, lives of saints, and theological themes. The detailed artistry of these frescoes provides insight into Byzantine religious beliefs and artistic styles. Notable churches featuring these frescoes include:

1. Apple Church (Elmali Kilise): This cruciform church displays well-preserved frescoes of Christ and the Virgin Mary.

2. Tokali Church: Known for its central dome, this church features a variety of frescoes depicting biblical stories and saints.

3. Snake Church (Yılanlı Kilise): Named for its depiction of Saint George slaying a dragon, this church has unique frescoes of various saints and religious scenes.

4. Dark Church (Karanlık Kilise): Renowned for its exceptionally well-preserved frescoes, this dimly lit church showcases the vibrant colours and artistry of the Byzantine era. An additional entrance fee is required to visit this church.

Exploring the Monastic Complex

The Göreme Open-Air Museum is more than a collection of churches. It includes a monastic complex with structures that support the religious community's daily needs. Visitors can explore refectories (dining halls), kitchens, and even rock-carved tombs, gaining a deeper understanding of the monks' daily lives and rituals.

* * *

Fairy Chimneys

Cappadocia's landscape is a sight to behold, with its enchanting Fairy Chimneys standing as the most whimsical and otherworldly features. These towering rock formations, also known as hoodoos or earth pyramids, have fascinated people for centuries with their unique appearance and geological origins.

Millions of years ago, volcanic eruptions from Mount Erciyes, Mount Hasan, and Mount Güllü covered the region with ash. Over time, wind and rain eroded these volcanic deposits, sculpting them into the dramatic rock formations seen today. The softer ash layers eroded more quickly, while the harder volcanic rock at the top remained, forming the distinctive mushroom-shaped caps of the Fairy Chimneys.

The soft volcanic rock of the Fairy Chimneys offered an ideal medium for human ingenuity. As early as the Hittite era (around 1600 BC), the inhabitants of Cappadocia began carving dwellings and places of worship into the rock faces. These remarkable feats of engineering transformed the Fairy Chimneys from natural wonders into living quarters, churches, and even pigeon houses.

Exploring the Varieties of Fairy Chimneys

Cappadocia features a diverse range of Fairy Chimneys, each with unique characteristics:

1. Pencil Chimneys: Tall and slender, these formations resemble giant pencils pointing skyward.

2. Twin Fairy Chimneys: Standing side-by-side, these formations often look like couples or siblings.

3. Split Fairy Chimneys: These have been split vertically, creating a dramatic and precarious appearance.

4. Multi-Tiered Fairy Chimneys: With multiple layers of erosion, these impressive formations resemble wedding cakes.

Several regions in Cappadocia offer stunning views of Fairy Chimneys:

1. Göreme Open-Air Museum: A UNESCO World Heritage Site with a high concentration of Fairy Chimneys, many carved into churches and monastic dwellings.

2. Devrent Valley (Imagination Valley): Known for Fairy Chimneys with unusual shapes that resemble animals and other figures, sparking the imagination.

3. Pasabag Valley (Monks Valley): Home to some of the most iconic Fairy Chimneys, including the Three Graces, a cluster of three striking formations.

4. Uchisar: A historic town atop a massive Fairy Chimney, offering panoramic views of the surrounding landscape.

* * *

Hot Air Balloon Ride

Experiencing Cappadocia from a hot air balloon is often considered the highlight of any visit to this enchanting region. Imagine gently floating through the sky at sunrise, with the first light of day casting a golden hue over the surreal landscape. The stunning views, tranquil atmosphere, and awe-inspiring scenery make a hot air balloon ride an unforgettable adventure.

What to Expect
1. Early Start: Balloon rides typically occur at sunrise, so be ready for an early wake-up call. The cooler morning air provides ideal conditions for ballooning.

2. Gentle Ascent: After a safety briefing, you'll step into the balloon's wicker

basket. As the pilot ignites the burners, you'll experience a gentle lift-off, slowly ascending into the sky.

3. Panoramic Views: As you rise, Cappadocia's mesmerising landscape unfolds below you. View the iconic Fairy Chimneys from a unique vantage point, marvel at vast valleys shaped by time, and spot hidden cave churches nestled in the cliffs.

4. Serene Journey: Unlike aeroplanes, hot air balloons move with the wind, offering a peaceful and silent experience. Enjoy the gentle whoosh of the burners and the breathtaking panoramic views.

5. Spectacular Light Show: Witness the stunning play of light and shadow as the sun bathes the landscape in golden hues. The changing colours and vistas create a breathtaking visual spectacle.

6. Celebratory Toast: Many balloon rides end with a celebratory toast of champagne or a traditional Turkish drink as you gently descend back to earth.

Considerations

1. Book in Advance: Hot air balloon rides are very popular in Cappadocia, so booking in advance is crucial, especially during peak season.
2. Safety First: Choose a reputable company with a strong safety record and experienced pilots.
3. Weather Dependent: Balloon flights are weather dependent and may be cancelled due to high winds, rain, or fog.
4. Duration and Cost: Balloon rides typically last one to two hours. Prices vary based on the company, duration, and amenities offered.

* * *

Pigeon Valley (Güvercinlik Vadisi)

Pigeon Valley, or Güvercinlik Vadisi in Turkish, is a captivating valley located between the towns of Göreme and Uçhisar in Cappadocia. This unique landscape is renowned not only for its dramatic rock formations but also for its rich history and cultural significance.

A Valley of Pigeon Holes

The name "Pigeon Valley" comes from the numerous man-made dovecotes carved into the soft volcanic rock of the valley's fairy chimneys. These pigeon houses served a practical purpose beyond their aesthetic appeal.

For centuries, locals used pigeons as a source of food and fertiliser. The nutrient-rich pigeon droppings collected from these dovecotes were used to enhance the fertility of the region's volcanic soil. Although chemical fertilisers are more common today, some farmers still maintain their dovecotes, attributing the sweetness of Cappadocia's grapes to these traditional fertilisation methods.

A Haven for Hikers and Photographers

Pigeon Valley is a paradise for outdoor enthusiasts. The 2.8-mile (4-kilometre) trail that winds through the valley offers breathtaking views of the landscape. Hikers will be enthralled by the towering fairy chimneys, dotted with pigeon holes, and the stunning vistas at every turn.

For a more adventurous experience, consider horse riding tours or jeep safaris to explore the valley's hidden gems. Look for historical remnants like abandoned rock-cut churches and cave dwellings, which offer a glimpse into a bygone era. An unforgettable way to experience Pigeon Valley is from a hot air balloon ride. Soaring through the sky, you can witness the valley's unique formations spread out beneath you, offering a truly awe-inspiring perspective.

* * *

Uchisar Castle

Towering over the town of Uchisar, Uchisar Castle (Uçhisar Kalesi) is a magnificent and historic landmark that has stood as a silent sentinel, guarding the Cappadocian landscape for centuries. Uchisar Castle is not your typical mediaeval structure. It is a natural citadel carved into a giant volcanic tuff cone, a type of soft rock formed from volcanic ash. Early inhabitants utilised these geological formations, hollowing out caves, rooms, and tunnels to create a formidable defensive complex.

The origins of Uchisar Castle are somewhat mysterious, but archaeological evidence suggests it was used as a stronghold as early as the Hittite period (around 1600 BC). Over the centuries, various civilizations, including the Romans, Byzantines, and Seljuk Turks, made modifications and fortifications to the castle.

Exploring the Castle's Depths

Climbing Uchisar Castle is an adventure. Narrow passageways wind through the rock, leading to various chambers and lookout points. As you ascend, you can see the ingenious use of space by past inhabitants.

The summit of Uchisar Castle offers breathtaking panoramic views of the entire Cappadocian landscape. From this vantage point, you can marvel at honeycombed cliffs, fairy chimneys, and sprawling valleys, all illuminated by golden sunlight. Historically, Uchisar Castle served as a watchtower, its strategic location allowing inhabitants to spot approaching dangers from afar. Today, it serves as a beacon for travellers, inviting them to explore its fascinating depths and enjoy unparalleled views.

Uchisar Castle is a must-see for anyone visiting Cappadocia. History enthusiasts will be captivated by its rich past, while adventure seekers will enjoy the challenge of climbing to the top. Whether you are interested in its architectural marvels or the stunning panoramas, Uchisar Castle promises an unforgettable experience.

* * *

Derinkuyu Underground City

Dive into the captivating world beneath the surface with a visit to Derinkuyu Underground City, an engineering marvel and testament to human ingenuity. Located near the town of Derinkuyu in Nevşehir Province, Turkey, this subterranean metropolis is one of the best-preserved underground cities in the world.

Derinkuyu, meaning "Deep Well" in Turkish, is thought to have been carved out of soft volcanic rock between the 7th and 8th centuries BC, though some believe it may date back even further. Initially used for storage and habitation, the city was significantly expanded during the Byzantine era (4th-15th centuries AD) to serve as a refuge from Arab and Mongol invasions.

A Masterpiece of Design

Derinkuyu reaches an impressive depth of approximately 280 feet (85 metres), with an intricate network of tunnels, chambers, and living spaces extending over 18 stories. Carved entirely by hand, the city showcases meticulous planning and construction techniques.

Life Underground

The residents of Derinkuyu adapted remarkably well to their subterranean environment. They carved homes, stables, storage rooms, wineries, a school, and a chapel into the volcanic rock. Ventilation shafts provided fresh air, while ingenious water collection systems ensured a constant water supply. Massive circular stone doors, weighing tons, served as security measures, sealing off the city from invaders.

Today, visitors can explore a portion of Derinkuyu, offering a glimpse into this fascinating era. Descend into the depths to marvel at the well-preserved living spaces, stables, and storage areas. Imagine the lives of those who sought refuge here, their daily routines, and the sense of community that thrived beneath the surface.

* * *

Kaymakli Underground City

Cappadocia's subterranean marvels extend beyond the famed Derinkuyu Underground City. Located in the town of Kaymaklı, the Kaymakli Underground City offers a captivating look into an era where creativity met the need for sanctuary.

Kaymakli was first carved out of soft volcanic rock by the Hittites as early as the 7th century BC and later expanded by early Christians fleeing religious persecution. It's believed that this underground city could accommodate up to 3,500 people! The city spans eight levels, though only four are open to the public, featuring an intricate network of tunnels, rooms, and corridors.

Journey into the Past

Entering Kaymakli is like stepping back in time. Steep, narrow passageways, designed to slow down invaders, take you deeper into the underground city. Watch for the iconic round millstones, which were cleverly used to block tunnels and thwart pursuers.

Life Below the Surface

Kaymakli was remarkably self-sufficient. Stables housed livestock, storage areas were stocked with provisions, and kitchens with hearths, disguised ventilation shafts, and even wineries supported long-term habitation.

The most striking feature of Kaymakli is its sophisticated design and engineering. The ventilation system, vital for breathable air, was a technical wonder. Hidden escape routes provided crucial exits during emergencies.

Today, Kaymakli offers a unique chance to explore a historical wonder. As you wander through the underground city, you can imagine the lives of those who once sought refuge there. Local guides offer valuable insights into the history and functionality of the various rooms.

Important Tips

1. Due to narrow passageways and uneven terrain, Kaymakli may not be suitable for those with claustrophobia or mobility issues.
2. Wear comfortable shoes with good grip for navigating uneven surfaces.
3. The underground temperature is cooler than above ground, so bring a light sweater.

4. Photography is allowed, but avoid using flash to protect the artefacts.

* * *

Paşabağı (Monks Valley)

Among Cappadocia's many striking landscapes, Paşabağı, also known as Monks Valley, stands out. This unique valley is famous for its towering fairy chimneys and its historical significance as a sanctuary for early Christians.

Paşabağı's most notable feature is its impressive array of fairy chimneys. These towering rock formations, shaped by millions of years of volcanic activity and erosion, look like giant mushrooms or fantastical chimneys. Unlike other valleys in Cappadocia, Paşabağı has a higher concentration of these formations, with some featuring double or even triple "chimneys" stacked on top of each other.

The soft volcanic rock of Paşabağı made it ideal for carving. During the early Byzantine era (4th-7th centuries AD), Christian monks and hermits found refuge in this secluded valley. They carved out dwellings and chapels, creating a monastic community that lasted for centuries.

Exploring the Monastic Complex
Among the most intriguing remnants in Paşabağı are the cave churches and hermitages. A notable example is the Çavuşin Church, a three-story structure with a cruciform plan and religious frescoes on its walls. Visitors can also explore smaller dwellings, some with narrow staircases leading to chapels at the tops of the fairy chimneys.

Paşabağı offers a unique mix of natural beauty and historical significance. Walking through the valley, surrounded by the towering rock formations, you can imagine the lives of the monks who once lived there. Climbing into some of the accessible dwellings provides a glimpse into their simple, spiritual existence.

Tips for Visiting Paşabağı

1. Paşabağı is near Göreme and easily accessible by car or tour bus.
2. There is a small entrance fee to visit the site.
3. Wear comfortable shoes for navigating uneven terrain.
4. Bring a hat and sunscreen, as there is limited shade.
5. Combine your visit with nearby attractions like Zelve Open Air Museum or Uchisar Castle for a full day of exploration.

* * *

Ihlara Valley

Within Cappadocia's rugged volcanic landscape, the Ihlara Valley is a stunning 16-kilometre (10-mile) gorge shaped by the Melendiz River. This valley seamlessly blends natural beauty, historical depth, and peaceful tranquillity.

The Ihlara Valley was formed millions of years ago by volcanic eruptions in the region. Over time, the Melendiz River carved through the soft volcanic tuff, creating the dramatic canyon walls that define the valley today. Lush vegetation flourishes along the riverbanks, contrasting beautifully with the stark rock formations.

A Refuge for Early Christians

From the 4th to the 13th centuries, the Ihlara Valley served as a sanctuary for persecuted Christians. Utilising the naturally formed caves and cliffs, they created numerous rock-cut churches and dwellings. These hidden sanctuaries became centres of worship and refuge, providing insight into the lives of early Christian communities.

Exploring the Valley

Hiking is the best way to experience the Ihlara Valley. The well-maintained trail follows the riverbank, offering stunning views of the gorge and lush greenery. Along the path, you'll find rock-cut churches adorned with frescoes depicting biblical scenes. Highlights include:

1. Kokar Church: Known for its intricate frescoes, including depictions of the Last Supper and the Virgin Mary, though partially blocked by a landslide.
2. Suyuncura Church: Features a well-preserved entrance hall and burial chamber, accessible after a short climb.
3. Kirkdamaltı Church: Also known as the Church Under the Trees, it is adorned with red, yellow, and green frescoes and is uniquely situated amid lush foliage.

The Ihlara Valley offers more than historical sites. You can enjoy a refreshing dip in the Melendiz River, perfect for cooling off on a hot day. The valley is also home to diverse birdlife, and you might spot turtles and frogs along the riverbanks. For a complete experience, consider a local lunch at a riverside restaurant, enjoying delicious Turkish cuisine amidst the valley's breathtaking scenery.

Planning Your Visit

The Ihlara Valley is accessible from the villages of Ihlara or Selime. Several tour operators offer guided hikes, or you can explore independently following the well-marked trail. Comfortable walking shoes are essential, and don't forget sunscreen, water, and a hat, especially during the hot summer months.

The Ihlara Valley offers a unique chance to explore Cappadocia's natural beauty, historical importance, and serene atmosphere. Lace up your hiking boots, embrace the adventure, and prepare to be captivated by this hidden gem.

* * *

Selime Monastery

Carved into the volcanic rock near the southern end of the Ihlara Valley, Selime Monastery stands as a testament to human ingenuity and enduring faith. Often referred to as Selime Castle (Selime Kalesi), this massive complex is more than a monastery; it is a labyrinth of chambers, churches, stables, and living quarters, making it the largest religious structure in Cappadocia.

The origins of Selime Monastery are somewhat mysterious. While evidence suggests a Hittite presence, its most significant development occurred during the Byzantine era, between the 8th and 11th centuries. Monks seeking refuge and a place for prayer transformed existing caves into an extensive monastic complex.

Exploring the Monastery

Selime Monastery is a multi-level marvel best explored with sturdy walking shoes and a sense of adventure. Here's what you can expect:

1. The Entrance: Ascend the steps carved into the rock face to the impressive entrance, featuring a relief of Saint George slaying a dragon.

2. The Upper Courtyard: This level houses the Basilica Church, a cathedral-sized space with two rows of rock columns dividing it into three sections. Look up at the barrel-vaulted ceiling and the remnants of frescoes depicting biblical scenes, though many details have been obscured by weathering and later use.

3. The Lower Courtyard: This area contains a network of tunnels, stables with carved-out feeding troughs, kitchens with massive chimneys, and storage chambers. Imagine the monks' lives as they carved out a place of worship and community within the volcanic rock.

4. The Church with the Cross-Patterned Ceiling: Located in the lower courtyard, this smaller church is notable for its intricate cross-patterned ceiling and geometric red and white decorations on the pillars.

5. The Tomb of Suleiman: Adjacent to the monastery complex lies the tomb of Suleiman, a Seljuk Sultan from the 13th century. This octagonal structure uniquely blends Islamic and Byzantine architectural styles.

Selime Monastery offers more than historical and architectural marvels; it provides a window into the lives of early Christians. Their dedication to faith and remarkable ability to adapt and thrive in a challenging environment is evident in the faded frescoes and worn carvings that whisper tales of a bygone era.

Important Tips

1. Wear sturdy shoes as the terrain can be uneven.
2. Be mindful of your head in the lower levels with lower ceilings.
3. Carry a flashlight or headlamp to navigate darker areas of the complex.
4. Photography is permitted, but be respectful of the site's religious signifi-

cance.

Chapter 3: Exploring Cappadocia Culture

Traditional Turkish Cuisine

E mbark on a delightful culinary journey through the rich tapestry of traditional Turkish cuisine, where Cappadocia serves as the perfect backdrop blending Ottoman heritage, Central Asian influences, and the freshness of local ingredients.

Here are some must-try dishes

1. Meze: It's the heart of Turkish dining, offering a variety of small plates for sharing. Dive into a selection of dips like hummus, baba ganoush, and spicy tomato paste alongside stuffed grape leaves, fried calamari, and creamy cheeses. Prices are usually budget-friendly, ranging from 10-20 Turkish Lira per plate.

2. Göme Bebek (Stuffed Baby Pigeon): A Cappadocian specialty featuring tender baby pigeons stuffed with a flavorful mix of rice, bulgur wheat, spices, and herbs. Though slightly pricier at around 30-40 TRY per serving, it's worth the taste experience.

3. Manti (Turkish Ravioli): These delectable dumplings filled with seasoned ground lamb or vegetarian options are topped with yoghourt sauce, paprika oil, and mint, priced around 20-30 TRY per serving.

4. Iskender Kebap: Thinly sliced, marinated grilled lamb layered over pita bread, smothered in tomato sauce, and topped with melted butter and yogurt. Prices usually range from 30-40 TRY per serving.

5. Lahmacun (Turkish Pizza): A thin-crust flatbread topped with seasoned ground lamb or minced meat, vegetables, and herbs, perfect for a quick and satisfying meal at around 10-15 TRY per serving.

6. Kumpir (Baked Potato): A giant baked potato loaded with various fillings like sausage, cheese, and vegetables, priced between 15-20 TRY depending on toppings.

To truly savour authentic flavours, explore local eateries favoured by Turks, often indicated by Turkish signage. These hidden gems offer a genuine taste of traditional cuisine and warm hospitality.

Don't miss the vibrant energy of local markets, where you can sample fresh olives, cheeses, and fruits, or pick up spices and Turkish delight. Opt for street food options like gözleme, simit, or döner kebabs for a quick, budget-friendly meal.

End your culinary adventure with sweet treats like Turkish delights, baklava, or rice pudding, priced around 5-10 TRY per piece. With each dish, you'll create lasting memories of the captivating flavours found in Cappadocia.

* * *

Must-Try Local Dishes

Embark on a delectable journey through Cappadocia with our guide to the must-try local dishes! Get ready to tantalise your taste buds with unique flavours and ancient culinary traditions. Here's what you shouldn't miss, along with estimated prices and suggestions on where to find them:

1. Testi Kebab (Pottery Kebab): Experience this iconic dish where tender lamb or beef is slow-cooked with vegetables inside a sealed clay pot, cracked open tableside to reveal succulent meat and a flavorful broth. Look for it at local restaurants, especially in villages like Avanos and Urgup, priced around ₺75-120 per person.

2. Çömlek Fasulye (Beans in a Pot): Vegetarians will love this hearty stew of white beans simmered with spices and tomato paste in a clay pot. Find it on menus at local eateries throughout Cappadocia, priced approximately ₺40-60 per serving.

3. Ayva Dolması (Stuffed Quince): Indulge in this seasonal delight featuring quince stuffed with a spiced mixture of rice, meat, and nuts, slowly simmered for a sweet and savory treat, priced around ₺50-80 per serving.

4. Kuru Kaymak (Dried Cream): Start your day with this unique breakfast item, buffalo milk cream air-dried for a thick, spreadable texture, perfect with honey or molasses, priced around ₺20-30 per portion.

5. Manti (Turkish Dumplings): Enjoy these delectable dumplings filled with lamb or beef and topped with yoghourt sauce and spiced butter, available at local restaurants for approximately ₺30-50 per serving.

6. Gözleme: Try this savoury flatbread filled with various ingredients like meat, cheese, or spinach, cooked until golden brown and crispy, priced around ₺15-25 per serving from vendors throughout Cappadocia.

7. Nevşehir Tandır (Tandoor Bread): Savour this fluffy, charred flatbread baked in a tandoor oven, perfect for dipping or enjoying on its own, available at local bakeries and vendors in Nevşehir for ₺5-10 per loaf.

8. Local Wines: Explore Cappadocia's flourishing wine industry with varieties like Emir and Öküzgözü, available at restaurants and wineries for tasting and tours (prices vary).

Remember, prices are approximate and can vary based on location and season. So, embrace the culinary adventure, delve into Cappadocia's rich culture, and create lasting memories through its diverse flavours!

* * *

Festivals and Events

Cappadocia's vibrant culture extends far beyond its historical sites and stunning landscapes. Throughout the year, the region bursts with a variety of festivals and events, offering a peek into local traditions and the warm hospitality of the Turkish people.

Here's a glimpse into some of the most popular Cappadocian festivals and events:

1. Cappadocia International Art Festival (Estimated Dates: June - July): Dive into a celebration of creativity as talented artists from around the globe showcase their work in painting, sculpture, photography, and performance art. Enjoy workshops, demonstrations, and exhibitions set in unique venues like cave churches and open-air museums.

2. Cappadocia Balloon Fest (Estimated Dates: Mid-July): Marvel at the spectacle of hundreds of colourful hot air balloons filling the skies at sunrise, offering unparalleled views of the region's iconic landscapes.

3. Hacı Bektaş Veli Commemoration Ceremonies and Culture and Art Festival (Estimated Dates: Late August): Join in the vibrant celebration of Turkish culture with traditional music, dance performances, artisan crafts, and culinary delights, all in honour of the revered Sufi mystic, Hacı Bektaş Veli.

4. Avanos Ceramics Festival (Estimated Dates: Early September): Explore the town's rich pottery-making heritage with demonstrations by skilled artisans, browsing through a myriad of ceramic creations, and even trying your hand at pottery making.

5. Urgup Vineyard Festival (Estimated Dates: September - October): Indulge in the region's flourishing wine scene with tastings, harvest activities, and delectable Turkish cuisine paired perfectly with local wines.

Beyond these major festivals, smaller local celebrations take place throughout the year in various towns and villages, offering a chance to experience authentic Turkish culture up close.

Tips for attending Cappadocia's festivals and events

1. Plan ahead: Book accommodations well in advance, as popular festivals can lead to fully booked hotels.

2. Embrace the crowds: Expect lively atmospheres and potential wait times for activities or transportation.

3. Dress comfortably: Wear suitable attire for outdoor events and comfortable shoes for walking.

4. Respect local customs: Remember to dress modestly and be mindful of local

traditions.

5. Bring cash: Some vendors may not accept credit cards, so it's wise to have Turkish Lira on hand.

Chapter 4: Accommodations in Cappadocia

Hotels and Resorts

These hotels and resorts offer a range of accommodations to suit different preferences and budgets, allowing visitors to experience the unique charm and beauty of Cappadocia in comfort and style.

1. Museum Hotel: Museum Hotel is a luxury cave hotel offering breathtaking views of the Cappadocian landscape. Each room is uniquely designed with antique furnishings and modern amenities. The hotel features a gourmet restaurant, spa, and outdoor swimming pool.

- Location: Göreme, Nevşehir
- Price per night: $300 - $800

2. Argos in Cappadocia: Argos in Cappadocia is a historic hotel set within the ancient caves of Uçhisar Castle. It offers luxurious rooms with panoramic views of the valley. Guests can enjoy fine dining at the hotel's restaurant and relax in the spa facilities.

- Location: Uçhisar, Nevşehir
- Price per night: $350 - $900

3. Kayakapi Premium Caves - Cappadocia: Kayakapi Premium Caves is a boutique hotel located in the UNESCO World Heritage site of Kayakapi. The hotel features beautifully restored cave dwellings with modern amenities. Guests can unwind in the hotel's spa or explore the nearby historic sites.

- Location: Ürgüp, Nevşehir
- Price per night: $250 - $700

4. Sultan Cave Suites: Sultan Cave Suites offers charming cave accommodations with stunning views of Göreme. The hotel's spacious rooms are elegantly decorated and equipped with modern comforts. Guests can enjoy traditional Turkish cuisine at the hotel's terrace restaurant.

- Location: Göreme, Nevşehir
- Price per night: $150 - $400

5. Cappadocia Cave Resort & Spa: Cappadocia Cave Resort & Spa is a luxury resort situated in the heart of Cappadocia. The resort boasts elegant cave rooms and suites, a world-class spa, and multiple dining options. Guests can also take part in activities such as hot air balloon rides and horseback riding.

- Location: Ürgüp, Nevşehir
- Price per night: $200 - $600

6. Taskonaklar Boutique Hotel: Taskonaklar Boutique Hotel is a charming boutique hotel located in the historic village of Ürgüp. The hotel offers cosy cave rooms and suites with modern amenities. Guests can enjoy stunning views of the surrounding landscape from the hotel's terrace.

- Location: Ürgüp, Nevşehir

- Price per night: $120 - $300

7. Kelebek Special Cave Hotel: Kelebek Special Cave Hotel is a family-run hotel set in a restored cave house in Göreme. The hotel features cosy cave rooms and suites decorated with traditional Turkish rugs and furnishings. Guests can relax in the hotel's garden or enjoy a Turkish bath experience.

- Location: Göreme, Nevşehir
- Price per night: $100 - $250

8. Rox Cappadocia: Rox Cappadocia is a modern boutique hotel located in the heart of Göreme. The hotel offers stylish rooms and suites with panoramic views of the fairy chimneys. Guests can enjoy a range of amenities including a rooftop terrace, spa, and Turkish bath.

- Location: Göreme, Nevşehir
- Price per night: $150 - $350

9. Esbelli Evi Cave Hotel: Esbelli Evi Cave Hotel is a charming family-run hotel housed in a restored Greek mansion in Ürgüp. The hotel offers cosy cave rooms and suites, each uniquely decorated with traditional Turkish textiles and furnishings. Guests can enjoy homemade Turkish breakfasts in the hotel's courtyard.

- Location: Ürgüp, Nevşehir
- Price per night: $100 - $250

10. Mithra Cave Hotel: Mithra Cave Hotel is a boutique hotel located in the historic village of Ürgüp. The hotel offers comfortable cave rooms and suites

with modern amenities. Guests can enjoy panoramic views of the surrounding valleys from the hotel's terrace.

- Location: Ürgüp, Nevşehir
- Price per night: $80 - $200

* * *

Rental Apartments

Rental apartments in Cappadocia offer travellers a unique and comfortable accommodation option, providing more space and privacy compared to traditional hotels. These apartments are often situated within cave dwellings or renovated historic buildings, blending modern amenities with the region's ancient charm. Guests can enjoy fully furnished units with kitchens, living areas, and sometimes even private terraces or balconies overlooking the stunning Cappadocian landscapes.

Location

Rental apartments are scattered throughout the various towns and villages of Cappadocia, including Göreme, Ürgüp, and Uchisar. They are conveniently located near major attractions, restaurants, and transportation hubs, allowing guests to easily explore the region's wonders.

Price per Night

The price per night for rental apartments in Cappadocia can vary depending on factors such as location, size, amenities, and seasonality. On average, guests can expect to pay between $50 to $150 USD per night for a comfortable and well-appointed apartment. Prices may fluctuate during peak tourist seasons, such as spring and fall when Cappadocia experiences the highest influx of visitors. Additionally, booking in advance or opting for longer stays may offer discounts or special rates.

Sample Rental Apartments

1. Cave Suite in Göreme: This charming cave suite offers a unique accommodation experience, featuring traditional stone walls and modern comforts. The suite includes a spacious bedroom, fully equipped kitchenette, and a cosy living area. Guests can enjoy panoramic views of the fairy chimney rock formations from the private terrace.

- Location: Göreme town centre, within walking distance of the Göreme Open-Air Museum.
- Price per Night: $80 USD

2. Historic Apartment in Ürgüp: Located in a renovated historic building, this apartment blends Ottoman architecture with contemporary design. The apartment boasts two bedrooms, a stylish living room, a fully equipped kitchen, and a dining area. Guests can relax on the rooftop terrace while admiring the sunset over the picturesque town of Ürgüp.

- Location: Central Ürgüp, close to restaurants, shops, and local attractions.
- Price per Night: $100 USD

3. Countryside Retreat in Uchisar: Escape the hustle and bustle of city life at this tranquil countryside retreat. The apartment features a rustic-chic interior with wooden furnishings and stone accents. Guests can unwind in the spacious bedroom, prepare meals in the modern kitchen, and dine al fresco on the private garden patio.

- Location: Uchisar village, surrounded by vineyards and orchards, with easy access to hiking trails and natural landmarks.
- Price per Night: $120 USD

These sample rental apartments showcase the diverse range of accommodation options available in Cappadocia, catering to different preferences and budgets. Whether you're seeking a cosy cave dwelling or a spacious countryside retreat, rental apartments offer a comfortable and memorable stay in this enchanting region.

Chapter 5: Day Trips and Excursions

Avanos

B eside the flowing waters of the Kizilirmak River, Avanos beckons travellers seeking an authentic experience away from Cappadocia's typical tourist hubs. With its rich history, natural beauty, and renowned pottery-making tradition, this charming town offers a unique glimpse into the region's cultural tapestry.

Formerly known as Venessa in ancient times, Avanos held significant importance in the Kingdom of Cappadocia. Explore remnants of its storied past, such as the impressive Saruhan Caravanserai, a 17th-century stopover for Silk Road travellers.

For history enthusiasts, the Guray Museum is a treasure trove of artefacts, offering insights into past civilizations.

A Haven for Pottery Enthusiasts

Avanos' hallmark is its age-old pottery tradition, fueled by the rich red clay deposited by the Kizilirmak River. Stroll through narrow streets lined with workshops, where skilled artisans craft pottery using time-honoured techniques. From dainty teacups to intricate decorative pieces, the array of pottery showcases centuries of craftsmanship.

Many workshops invite visitors to witness pottery-making demonstrations, and some even offer hands-on experiences. Trying your hand at the pottery wheel is a delightful activity for all ages, with the chance to take home a one-of-a-kind souvenir.

While pottery takes centre stage, Avanos offers more to explore. Wander through its scenic streets, visit charming mosques, or enjoy a leisurely stroll along the riverbank. Adventurous souls can venture into nearby valleys or ascend the ancient rock castle of Uchisar for panoramic views.

Avanos delights food lovers with its vibrant culinary scene, featuring Turkish specialties like gözleme and keşkek, alongside local wines from the surrounding vineyards. Avanos' central location makes it an ideal starting point for exploring Cappadocia's wonders, from Göreme's cave churches to Ürgüp's fairy chimneys. Consider adding a hot air balloon ride for a truly unforgettable experience.

* * *

Ortahisar

While Göreme and Uchisar often hog the limelight, Cappadocia harbours a trove of hidden treasures waiting to be uncovered. Enter Ortahisar, a quaint town nestled amidst the enchanting landscapes, promising an authentic glimpse into Turkish life and a slice of Cappadocia's lesser-known history.

Ortahisar Castle

Standing tall against the skyline is the majestic Ortahisar Castle, a monolithic wonder sculpted by nature and time. Once known as "Potamía" in Byzantine times, the castle served as a natural fortress and lookout point. Ascend its winding staircases (moderate fitness advised) to behold sweeping views of valleys and villages. Explore its chambers, once homes and storerooms.

Beyond the Castle

Ortahisar exudes a laid-back vibe compared to bustling Cappadocian hubs. Roam its cobblestone streets flanked by Ottoman houses, soak in local flavours, and engage with friendly locals.

Town Highlights

1. Abdioglu Camii: A 17th-century mosque showcasing Ottoman architecture.

2. Local Crafts: Discover traditional carpet weaving and pottery at local workshops.

3. Culinary Delights: Relish authentic Turkish cuisine at family-run eateries.

Ortahisar as a Base

Strategically located, Ortahisar serves as a gateway to Cappadocia's wonders. Plan day trips to Göreme Open-Air Museum, Uchisar Castle, or Ihlara Valley effortlessly. Ortahisar offers solace from the crowds, inviting you to immerse in its history and hospitality.

Tips for Exploring Ortahisar

1. Wear sturdy shoes for navigating cobblestone streets.
2. Visit the castle early or late to avoid midday heat.
3. Carry cash for smaller shops.
4. Learn basic Turkish phrases for enhanced interactions.

* * *

Soğanlı Valley

While Göreme and other bustling Cappadocian spots draw crowds, Soğanlı Valley offers a serene retreat brimming with history and natural splendour. Tucked away in Kayseri province's Yeşilhisar district, this valley, once known as Soandós, invites travellers in search of a quieter, off-the-beaten-path adventure.

Soğanlı Valley's roots run deep, tracing back to the Byzantine era. Early Christians carved intricate cave churches and monasteries into the volcanic rock, creating a hidden sanctuary adorned with frescoes depicting religious tales.

Exploring the Valley

Divided into Aşağı Soğanlı (Lower Soğanlı) and Yukarı Soğanlı (Upper Soğanlı), the valley is a treasure trove of discoveries. Wander through the charming streets of Aşağı Soğanlı, where traditional Turkish life unfolds, and encounter artisans crafting Soganli dolls.

Must-See Sights

1. Church of Saint Barbara (Tahtalı Kilise): Accessible by a wooden bridge, this church showcases barrel-vaulted architecture and rare frescoes.

2. Yılanlı Kilise (Snake Church): Explore this monastery, adorned with remnants of frescoes, including its namesake snakes.

3. Balıklı Kilise (Fish Church): Admire the baptismal pool adorned with fish carvings and serene frescoes.

Beyond the Churches

Hike along scenic trails, marvelling at dramatic rock formations and ancient pigeon houses dotting the cliffs. Soğanlı Valley offers solace away from the bustling tourist hubs. Immerse yourself in its peaceful ambiance, delve into its historic churches, and embrace the warmth of local hospitality.

Planning Your Visit

Prepare for a smaller-scale destination with limited amenities. Bring essentials like water and snacks, and consider hiring a local guide for enriched insights into the valley's history.

Soğanlı Valley is Perfect for

1. Travellers seeking off-the-beaten-path experiences
2. History enthusiasts exploring ancient churches and monasteries
3. Nature lovers embarking on scenic hikes
4. Anyone craving tranquillity away from the crowds

So, if you yearn for an authentic Cappadocian adventure immersed in history and serenity, Soğanlı Valley awaits your exploration.

* * *

Güzelyurt

On the outskirts of Cappadocia's rustic scenery, Güzelyurt beckons travellers in search of a serene refuge from the tourist bustle. Aptly named "Beautiful Land" in Turkish, this enchanting town invites exploration, boasting a rich tapestry of history, culture, and natural splendour.

Güzelyurt's allure lies in its diverse history, shaped by centuries of cross-cultural exchange. Greeks, Turks, Kurds, and Bulgarians have all woven their stories into the town's fabric, evident in its architecture where traditional Turkish dwellings blend with Byzantine remnants.

Unlike its bustling Cappadocian counterparts, Güzelyurt offers a quieter, more authentic experience. Immerse yourself in the unhurried rhythm of local life, engage with welcoming locals, and discover a different side of Cappadocia.

Exploring Güzelyurt's Gems

1. Monastery Valley: Delve into history at Monastery Valley, home to over 50 ancient cave churches dating back to the 7th century AD. While some are off-limits, their intricate details offer glimpses into the region's Christian past.

2. Ihlara Valley: Embark on a scenic hike through Ihlara Valley, a 14-kilometre canyon carved by the Melendiz River. Marvel at lush scenery, rock-cut churches, and traces of Cappadocia's Christian heritage.

3. Turkish Cuisine: Indulge in authentic Turkish flavours at local eateries, or join a cooking class to uncover the secrets behind these delectable dishes.

Güzelyurt's central location makes it a perfect hub for exploring nearby treasures like Aksaray's historical mosques or Göreme's iconic landscapes.

Tips for Güzelyurt

1. Limited Infrastructure: Be prepared for fewer tourist facilities. Brush up on basic Turkish or use translation apps for smoother interactions.

2. Accommodation: Opt for guesthouses or boutique hotels for an intimate, local stay.

3. Embrace the Pace: Embrace the relaxed vibe of Güzelyurt, and savour the genuine warmth of Turkish hospitality.

Chapter 6: Nightlife in Cappadocia

Bars and Clubs

W hile Cappadocia is famous for its rich history and stunning natural beauty, it also boasts a lively nightlife, especially in Göreme, Ürgüp, and Uchisar. Here's a glimpse into the diverse nighttime activities available:

1. Cave Bars: Immerse yourself in Cappadocia's unique landscape by enjoying a drink at one of its cave bars. Carved into volcanic rock, these atmospheric venues provide an unforgettable experience. Some popular options include:

2. The Ember Lounge (Göreme): Offering live music and a chic ambiance. (Estimated Hours: 8:00 PM - 2:00 AM, Entry Fee: Possible)

3. Ali Baba Restaurant & Cave Bar (Göreme): A lively spot with traditional Turkish music and a wide beverage selection. (Estimated Hours: 7:00 PM - 2:00 AM, Entry Fee: Possible)

4. Aziz Cave Restaurant (Uchisar): Delight in Turkish cuisine and local wines before experiencing the vibrant nightlife. (Estimated Hours: 6:00 PM - 2:00 AM, Entry Fee: Possible)

5. Rooftop Bars: For breathtaking views of Cappadocia's landscapes, head

to a rooftop bar. Sip cocktails while enjoying the starry sky and town lights. Options include:

1. The Pumpkin Restaurant & Bar (Göreme): Offering stunning views of fairy chimneys and hot air balloons. (Estimated Hours: 10:00 AM - Midnight, Entry Fee: Usually None)
2. Lithos Bar (Uchisar): Located atop Uchisar Castle, this bar offers panoramic views and a laid-back atmosphere. (Estimated Hours: Sunset - Midnight, Entry Fee: Possible)

Live Music Venues

Immerse yourself in local music at live venues, from traditional Turkish folk to contemporary bands. Popular choices include:

1. Sarıhan Caravanserai (Göreme): This historic venue often hosts live music performances. (Estimated Hours: Varies, Entry Fee: Possible)

2. The Argos in Cappadocia (Uchisar): A luxurious cave hotel with a sophisticated bar and occasional live music nights. (Estimated Hours: Varies, Entry Fee: Possible for Music Events)

Nightclubs

For those craving dance and excitement, nightclubs are available, mainly in Göreme. Examples include:

1. Club Afilli (Göreme): A popular spot with DJs and a lively dance floor. (Estimated Hours: 11:00 PM - 4:00 AM, Entry Fee: Applicable)
2. Club Aura (Göreme): Another vibrant option with DJs and a lively atmosphere. (Estimated Hours: 11:00 PM - 4:00 AM, Entry Fee: Applicable)

Important Notes

1. Operation hours and entry fees are estimates and may vary based on factors like season and events. Always check with the venue directly for accurate information.
2. The legal drinking age in Turkey is 18. ID may be required.
3. Some upscale venues may have dress code restrictions.

Cappadocia's nightlife offers a chance to relax after a day of exploration, mingle with locals and fellow travellers, and discover a different side of the region. Whether you prefer live music or dancing, Cappadocia's nighttime scene has something for everyone. Just remember to drink responsibly and savour the unique ambiance.

* * *

Theatres and Performing Arts

Though Cappadocia is famed for its historical marvels and natural beauty, it also boasts a dynamic performing arts scene. Here's a sneak peek into what's in store for you.

Theatrical Marvels

1. Mevlana Lodge Performances (Konya): While not in Cappadocia directly, no trip to the region is complete without witnessing the Whirling Dervishes Ceremony. Konya, just a two-hour drive from Göreme, hosts this mesmerising ritual at the Mevlana Lodge, the heart of the Mevlevi Order. Watch as dancers clad in flowing white robes perform, symbolising a spiritual connection with

the divine. Shows typically run on Tuesdays and Thursdays at 7:00 PM, with additional weekend performances during peak tourist times. Tickets range from 40 TL to 80 TL (about $5 to $10 USD).

2. Göreme Open-Air Museum Performances: In summer, the Göreme Open-Air Museum occasionally hosts theatrical events. These open-air shows feature historical reenactments, traditional dances, or plays set against Cappadocia's iconic rock formations. Showtimes and entry fees vary, so it's best to check with the museum or local tourist centres for details. Entry fees are usually separate from museum admission and may range from 20 TL to 50 TL (approximately $3 to $6 USD).

Cappadocia's performing arts scene goes beyond traditional theatre. Many restaurants and cafes, especially in Göreme and Ürgüp, host live music nights featuring local talents or bands. It's a great way to enjoy good food while immersing yourself in the local music scene.

Things to Keep in Mind

1. Limited Options: Cappadocia's theatre scene is smaller compared to big cities, so plan ahead as schedules may change.

2. Seasonal Availability: Most performances, especially outdoor ones, happen during the peak tourist season (April to October).

3. Ticket Purchase: You can usually buy tickets at the venue or through local travel agencies. Consider booking ahead for popular shows.

4. Dress Code: While there's usually no strict dress code, dressing modestly is advisable, especially when visiting religious sites or attending cultural events.

Although Cappadocia may not boast grand theatres, it offers unique experiences for those interested in the performing arts. From the enchanting Whirling Dervishes Ceremony to open-air shows in historical settings, there's something for every theatre enthusiast to explore.

Chapter 7: Shopping in Innsbruck

Markets and Boutiques

I n addition to its stunning landscapes and rich history, Cappadocia is a paradise for those who love shopping. From lively local markets packed with authentic treasures to quaint boutiques showcasing regional crafts, the area caters to various tastes and budgets.

Exploring the Bustling Markets

1. Göreme Open-Air Museum Market (Open Daily, 9:00 AM - 6:00 PM): Located near the iconic museum, this market offers a vibrant selection of souvenirs and local handicrafts. You can browse through carpets, rugs, pottery, jewellery, and textiles, all reflecting the unique style of Cappadocia.

2. Avanos Bazaar (Weekdays, 8:00 AM - 7:00 PM): Experience the lively atmosphere of Avanos Bazaar, famous for its red clay pottery. Watch skilled artisans at work and explore a wide range of handmade ceramic pieces, from intricate plates and vases to decorative ornaments. Don't forget to negotiate for the best deal!

3. Urgup Old Town Market (Weekdays, 8:00 AM - 7:00 PM): Step into Urgup's Old Town Market for a journey back in time. This charming market offers a diverse array of goods, including carpets, kilims, traditional clothing, spices, and local produce. Be sure to try some freshly baked Turkish delight, a sweet

treat synonymous with the region.

Discovering Unique Boutiques

For those in search of unique pieces and a more curated shopping experience, Cappadocia boasts a charming selection of boutiques. These stores feature the work of local artisans, specialising in handcrafted jewellery, handwoven textiles, traditional Turkish lamps, and carpets.

· Göreme: Wander the narrow streets of Göreme and stumble upon hidden gems like Caravana يارس (Caravanserai) or Kilimjilar Bazaar, where you'll find exquisite carpets and kilims.

· Uchisar: Explore Uchisar Castle and uncover boutiques nestled within the cave dwellings. These shops offer a treasure trove of handcrafted jewellery, scarves, and souvenirs with a local touch.

Operating Hours

· Markets: Most local markets in Cappadocia are open weekdays from 8:00 AM to 7:00 PM, with extended hours during peak tourist season. Some markets near tourist sites may open on weekends with shorter hours.

· Boutiques: Boutique hours vary, typically opening weekdays from 10:00 AM to 7:00 PM, with some staying open later in the summer. Always check specific timings at the store.

Shopping Tips in Cappadocia

1. Embrace Haggling: Negotiating prices is common in local markets. Research typical prices beforehand and be prepared to bargain for the best deal.

2. Cash is King: While some shops accept credit cards, it's advisable to carry Turkish Lira, especially at local markets.

3. Support Local Artisans: Look for shops showcasing the work of local artisans to support traditional crafts and the local economy.

4. Beware of Counterfeits: While most vendors sell genuine products, be cautious of imitations, especially for carpets and kilims. Ask for certificates of authenticity if unsure.

* * *

Souvenirs and Handicrafts

No Cappadocian journey is complete without a keepsake to treasure your memories. Beyond the typical tourist offerings, Cappadocia boasts a rich tradition of handicrafts, each piece carrying the region's cultural heritage and artistic legacy. Here's your go-to guide for finding that perfect memento:

1. Hand-Woven Carpets and Kilims: Immerse yourself in Cappadocia's vibrant textile tradition with a hand-woven carpet or kilim. Carpets are renowned for their intricate patterns and rich colours, while kilims feature flat-woven tapestries with geometric designs and symbolic motifs. Seek out kilims made

with natural dyes and local Anatolian wool for an authentic touch.

2. Onyx Jewelry and Stoneware: Discover the beauty of Cappadocian onyx, a semi-precious stone prized for its layered appearance. Local artisans fashion onyx into exquisite jewellery pieces like earrings, necklaces, and bracelets. You can also find decorative objects like vases, bowls, and chess sets carved from onyx, adding a touch of elegance to your home.

3. Hand-Painted Ceramics: Avanos, known for its pottery, is the place to find hand-painted ceramics. Explore the shops for a variety of pieces, from functional tableware to decorative vases and figurines adorned with traditional Turkish patterns or historical motifs.

4. Evil Eye Charms (Nazar Boncuk): A beloved Turkish souvenir, the Evil Eye Charm is a beautiful talisman believed to ward off negativity and bring good fortune. These hand-painted glass beads come in different colours and sizes, making them a delightful and affordable keepsake.

5. Turkish Delight: Treat yourself to authentic Turkish Delight (Lokum), a sweet confection made with sugar, starch, and flavours like rosewater, lemon, or pistachios. Pack a box to enjoy a taste of Cappadocia back home.

6. Cappadocia-Themed Crafts: Bring home a piece of Cappadocia's unique landscape with souvenirs featuring its iconic landmarks. Look for hand-painted plates or fridge magnets depicting Fairy Chimneys, hot air balloons, or historic cave churches.

Where to Find Souvenirs

1. Local Shops and Boutiques: Explore the quaint shops in Göreme, Avanos, and Uchisar for a wider selection of handcrafted items compared to touristy spots.

2. Caravanserais: These historic inns often host shops selling traditional

handicrafts and souvenirs.

3. Weekly Markets: Immerse yourself in the local scene at weekly markets, where you can find a variety of souvenirs, including handmade crafts and fresh produce, at reasonable prices.

Tips for Souvenir Shopping

1. Prioritise Quality: Opt for handcrafted pieces made with traditional techniques over mass-produced items.
2. Support Local Artisans: Choose shops that collaborate directly with local artisans to ensure fair compensation for their work.
3. Negotiate Respectfully: Bargaining is expected at markets and some shops, so negotiate politely and respectfully.
4. Consider Logistics: Keep in mind the weight and size of your souvenirs, especially for larger items like carpets, when planning for transportation.

Chapter 8: Outdoor Activities

Hiking and Trekking Routes

Cappadocia's enchanting landscapes beckon to be explored firsthand, inviting adventurers to lace up their hiking boots and embark on unforgettable journeys through valleys shaped by time, past hidden churches, and amidst breathtaking vistas.

Routes for Every Level

Cappadocia caters to hikers of all levels, offering trails ranging from leisurely strolls to challenging multi-day treks. Select a route that aligns with your fitness level, experience, and desired duration of adventure.

Short Hikes (1-3 hours)

1. Pigeon Valley Hike: Enjoy an easy and picturesque stroll through Pigeon Valley, named for its abundance of pigeon houses carved into the cliffs. Take in panoramic views of Uchisar Castle and the surrounding landscape.

2. Love Valley Hike: Explore the heart of Love Valley on this moderately challenging loop trail, renowned for its unique rock formations. Encounter fairy chimneys, carved churches, and awe-inspiring viewpoints along the way.

3. Red & Rose Valley Hike: Embark on a captivating journey through the Red and Rose Valleys, known for their vibrant rock formations. This moderate

loop trail offers stunning scenery and historical sites like the "Grape Church."

4. Göreme Panorama Hike: Take a short yet rewarding hike to a viewpoint overlooking Göreme Open Air Museum and the surrounding valleys. Witness the vastness of Cappadocia and capture breathtaking panoramic views.

Moderate Hikes (3-6 hours)

1. Ihlara Valley Hike: Follow the Melendiz River through the picturesque Ihlara Valley, a 14-kilometre canyon adorned with lush vegetation and numerous rock-cut churches. Experience a blend of nature and history on this scenic trail.

2. Zemi Valley Hike: Discover the hidden gem of Zemi Valley on this moderate hike. This lesser-known valley boasts dramatic rock formations, historical cave churches, and a tranquil ambiance.

Multi-Day Treks

For seasoned hikers seeking extended adventures, multi-day treks traversing Cappadocia's diverse landscapes are available. These treks often involve camping or staying in local guest houses along the route. Popular options include:

1. Serpent Valley Trek: Navigate through dramatic canyons, past secluded villages, and revel in stunning panoramic vistas on this challenging trek.

2. UzunDere Trek: Embark on a multi-day exploration of Cappadocia's longest river valley, featuring diverse flora and fauna, historical sites, and glimpses of local life.

Pre-Hike Considerations

1. Choose the Right Season: Optimal hiking conditions are typically found in spring and autumn, with mild temperatures. Summers can be hot, while winters may bring snow to some areas.

2. Gear and Attire: Wear sturdy hiking boots, weather-appropriate clothing, and don't forget sun protection like a hat and sunscreen.

3. Supplies: Carry ample water, snacks, sunscreen, insect repellent, and a first-aid kit.

4. Navigation: Bring along a detailed map or use a GPS app to navigate trails. Consider hiring a local guide for challenging hikes.

5. Safety: Stay on marked trails, watch out for loose rocks, and be mindful of wildlife encounters.

Respecting the Environment

1. Leave No Trace: Pack out all trash and avoid littering.
2. Respect Local Culture: Dress modestly near religious sites and in villages.
3. Support Local Communities: Opt for locally-owned accommodations and shops.

By adhering to these guidelines and selecting a route that suits your abilities, you'll embark on a rewarding and unforgettable hiking adventure in the heart of Cappadocia. So, strap on your boots, breathe in the fresh air, and prepare to discover Cappadocia's hidden treasures on foot.

* * *

Cycling Tours and E-Bike Rentals

Cappadocia's awe-inspiring landscapes, from majestic valleys to volcanic rock formations, beckon to be explored up close. Cycling, especially with the assistance of e-bikes, provides a thrilling and immersive way to discover the region's hidden treasures and witness its beauty firsthand.

Exploring Cappadocia on Two Wheels

Traditional Cycling Tours

1. Suitable for All Levels: Cycling tours in Cappadocia cater to a diverse range of fitness levels. Whether you prefer leisurely rides or off-road adventures, there's a route for everyone.

2. Uncovering Hidden Gems: Guided cycling tours unveil secret spots off the beaten path, offering glimpses of hidden valleys, quaint villages, and ancient sites inaccessible by car.

3. Cultural Immersion: Many tours include stops at local villages, providing opportunities to engage with residents and delve into the rich tapestry of Cappadocian culture and traditions.

4. Safety Measures: Reputable tour operators prioritise safety, providing experienced guides, safety briefings, and well-maintained bicycles for a worry-free experience.

The Advent of E-Bikes

1. Effortless Exploration: E-bikes revolutionise exploration by assisting riders with electric motors, making uphill climbs and long distances a breeze for cyclists of all abilities.

2. Embracing the Landscape: With e-bikes, riders can focus on soaking in the stunning scenery, from the unique rock formations to the sounds of nature,

without the distraction of exertion.

E-Bike Rental Options

1. Wide Selection: Numerous shops in key towns like Göreme, Ürgüp, and Avanos offer e-bike rentals, boasting various models to suit individual preferences.

2. Flexible Rentals: Choose from half-day or full-day rentals to embark on independent explorations or opt for guided tours provided by some rental shops.

Key Considerations

1. Safety Gear: Helmets are mandatory for cyclists in Turkey, typically provided by rental shops along with the bike.

2. Traffic Awareness: Adhere to traffic regulations and exercise caution, particularly on main roads. Utilise designated cycling paths whenever available.

3. Weather Awareness: Plan your ride according to weather conditions, avoiding extreme heat or heavy rain for a comfortable and enjoyable experience.

4. Fitness Level: While e-bikes enhance accessibility, a basic level of fitness is still beneficial. Select routes that align with your physical abilities for a rewarding adventure.

Cycling or e-biking through Cappadocia promises an unforgettable journey, offering a unique perspective on the region's allure. Embrace the fresh air, conquer scenic trails, and create lasting memories as you pedal through the enchanting landscapes of Cappadocia.

* * *

Horseback Riding through the Valleys

Cappadocia's surreal landscapes beckon to be experienced not just visually, but holistically. Picture yourself galloping through valleys sculpted by millennia of wind and water erosion, with the iconic Fairy Chimneys looming overhead. Horseback riding in Cappadocia offers a unique and exhilarating way to immerse yourself in this captivating region.

Saddle up and embark on a journey that transcends centuries. Cappadocia's horseback riding tours often follow ancient pathways once traversed by traders and travellers along the Silk Road. Envision caravans winding through these same routes, carrying goods and stories from distant lands.

Exploring Diverse Landscapes

Horseback riding grants access to areas beyond the reach of conventional vehicles, delving deeper into Cappadocia's valleys. Discover hidden nooks, meander through orchards, and behold panoramic vistas that will take your breath away. Select from tours exploring the dramatic terrain of Rose Valley, the historical significance of Sword Valley, or the surreal formations of Devrent Valley (Imagination Valley).

For Riders of All Levels

Whether you're an experienced equestrian or a novice rider, Cappadocia accommodates all skill levels. Most tour operators provide gentle Anatolian or Arabian horses prized for their docility and surefootedness. Seasoned guides assess your proficiency and tailor the ride to your comfort level, ensuring a safe and enjoyable experience.

Horseback riding in Cappadocia engages all your senses. Feel the rhythmic sway of the horse beneath you, breathe in the fragrance of wild herbs in the air, and listen to the symphony of nature amidst the tranquil landscapes. This multi-sensory immersion fosters a profound connection with the environment.

Choosing the Right Tour

With a variety of horseback riding tours available, consider the following factors when selecting your adventure:

1. Duration: Choose a tour that fits your schedule, whether it's a brief introductory ride or a full-day excursion.

2. Skill Level: Be honest about your riding experience to ensure a safe and enjoyable outing. Opt for beginner-friendly tours or more challenging options for seasoned riders.

3. Itinerary: Select a tour that aligns with your interests, whether you're drawn to specific valleys or desire a comprehensive exploration of Cappadocia's diverse terrain.

Enhancing Your Experience

1. Dress Appropriately: Wear long pants, sturdy closed-toe shoes, and comfortable attire suitable for riding. Don't forget sun protection like a hat and sunscreen.

2. Stay Hydrated: Carry water to stay hydrated, particularly during warm weather.

3. Embrace Adventure: Approach the experience with an open mind and a spirit of adventure. Horseback riding offers a unique perspective on Cappadocia's wonders.

Chapter 9: Planning Your Itinerary

A 7-Day General Itinerary

C appadocia, with its mesmerising landscapes, rich history, and vibrant culture, promises an unforgettable adventure. This 7-day general itinerary offers a framework for exploring the region's highlights while allowing room for personalization based on your interests and pace.

Day 1: Arrival and Settling In

- Arrive at Kayseri Airport or Nevşehir Kapadokya Airport and transfer to your hotel in Göreme, a central location offering easy access to attractions.
- Check in, freshen up, and explore Göreme's charming streets lined with shops, cafes, and restaurants.
- In the evening, savour a traditional Turkish dinner at a rooftop restaurant with panoramic valley views. (Overnight in Göreme)

Day 2: Unveiling Göreme Open-Air Museum and Exploring Uchisar

- Begin your day with a visit to the Göreme Open-Air Museum, a UNESCO World Heritage Site. Explore rock-cut churches adorned with vibrant frescoes depicting biblical scenes.
- In the afternoon, journey to Uchisar, Cappadocia's highest point. Climb

Uchisar Castle for breathtaking panoramic views of the valleys.
- In the evening, witness a whirling dervish ceremony in a historic cara-vanserai, immersing yourself in the mesmerising Sufi ritual. (Overnight in Göreme)

Day 3: Delving into Valleys and Underground Cities

- Embark on a full-day tour exploring Cappadocia's valleys.
- Discover the iconic Fairy Chimneys in Rose Valley, known for its rosy hues at sunrise or sunset.
- Hike through Love Valley, marvelling at its unique rock formations resembling chimneys with cone-shaped tops.
- Explore the mysterious underground city of Derinkuyu or Kaymakli, hidden networks used by early Christians.
- In the evening, join a traditional Turkish cooking class, learning local recipes and enjoying your creations. (Overnight in Göreme)

Day 4: Soaring Above the Landscape in a Hot Air Balloon

- Wake early for a hot air balloon ride over Cappadocia. Drift peacefully as the sun rises, witnessing breathtaking views of the valleys and Fairy Chimneys.
- Enjoy a champagne toast and breakfast after your flight.
- In the afternoon, visit a local carpet weaving workshop or explore the pottery shops in Avanos. (Overnight in Göreme)

Day 5: Venturing Beyond Göreme: Ihlara Valley and Selime Monastery

- Explore areas beyond Göreme. Hike through the scenic Ihlara Valley, marvelling at rock-cut churches nestled in the cliffs.

- Visit Selime Monastery, a breathtaking cave monastery offering stunning views of the landscape.
- Stop at Pasabag Valley, or Monks Valley, to see unique chimney formations and carved dwellings. (Overnight in Göreme)

Day 6: A Day of Leisure and Optional Activities

- Enjoy a leisurely day. Relax by the hotel pool, explore independently, or experience a Turkish hammam for relaxation.
- In the evening, savour a farewell dinner at a local restaurant with live music. (Overnight in Göreme)

Day 7: Departure

- Enjoy breakfast at your hotel before transferring to the airport for your departure flight, taking home cherished memories of your Cappadocian adventure.

Customise the itinerary based on your interests. Consider horseback riding tours, traditional Turkish night shows, or visits to Güzelyurt for a more traditional experience.

Remember

1. Book hot air balloon rides in advance, especially during peak seasons.
2. Purchase a Museum Pass for discounted entry to attractions.
3. Research dress codes for religious sites.
4. Pack comfortable shoes for walking.

* * *

A 7-Day Culinary Itinerary

Embark on an enticing journey through Cappadocia, where each meal is a celebration of fresh, seasonal ingredients and rich culinary traditions. This 7-day plan will delight your taste buds and introduce you to the unique flavours that define Cappadocian cuisine.

Day 1: Welcome to Cappadocia - Sampling Local Flavors

- Start your day with a traditional Turkish breakfast ("kahvaltı"), featuring an assortment of fresh cheeses, olives, cured meats, tomatoes, cucumbers, jams, honey, and freshly baked bread. Don't forget to try "menemen," a dish of scrambled eggs with tomatoes, peppers, and onions.
- Explore Göreme and treat yourself to a delicious "gözleme," a savoury flatbread filled with options like cheese, spinach, ground meat, or potatoes.
- Indulge in a "testi kebabı," a clay pot kebab slowly cooked with meat, vegetables, and spices, paired perfectly with local Turkish wine.

Day 2: Exploring Underground Tastes in Kaymaklı

- Enjoy a leisurely breakfast at your hotel, perhaps with fresh fruits and yoghourt.
- Delve into history with a unique lunch experience in Kaymaklı Underground City, where restaurants offer traditional Turkish meals in a memorable setting.
- In Ürgüp, try "mantı," small dumplings filled with meat or vegetables,

served with yoghourt sauce and spices, accompanied by a refreshing "ayran."

Day 3: A Day Trip to Avanos - Pottery and Cuisine

- Fuel up with a hearty breakfast, including "simit," a circular bread with sesame seeds.
- In Avanos, known for its pottery making tradition, enjoy lunch with a view and sample Turkish soups like lentil or tomato soup.
- Indulge in a spread of "meze," featuring appetisers like dolma, hummus, baba ganoush, and fried calamari, perfect for sharing.

Day 4: Hot Air Balloon Ride and a Lavish Lunch

- Start your day with breakfast before a breathtaking hot air balloon ride.
- Celebrate with a luxurious lunch at a cave hotel or upscale restaurant, savouring gourmet Turkish dishes or international cuisine with a local twist.

Day 5: Cooking Class and Home-Cooked Dinner

- Participate in a cooking class to learn classic Turkish dishes like "imam bayıldı" or "baklava."
- Enjoy your creations for lunch and experience Turkish hospitality with a home-cooked dinner hosted by a local family.

Day 6: A Farewell Feast in Ortahisar

- Relish a relaxed breakfast at your hotel, perhaps with "menemen" or fresh pastries.

- Explore Ortahisar and enjoy lunch with stunning views, opting for seafood dishes or classic Turkish pide.
- Celebrate your last night with a grand feast of grilled meats, kebabs, fresh salads, and traditional Turkish desserts like "künefe."

Day 7: Departure with Fond Memories

- Enjoy a final Turkish breakfast and pick up some local delicacies like "lokum" or baklava before departing Cappadocia. This itinerary sets the stage for your culinary adventure in Cappadocia.

* * *

A 7-Day Romantic Itinerary for Couples

Craft a romantic journey filled with unforgettable moments with this carefully curated 7-day itinerary tailored for couples seeking a captivating getaway to Cappadocia.

Day 1: Arrival and Romance Unveiled

- Morning: Touch down at Kayseri Airport or Nevşehir Kapadokya Airport and be whisked away to your enchanting cave hotel in Göreme.

- Afternoon: Relax and take in the breathtaking vistas of fairy chimneys and valleys from your private balcony.

- Evening: Delight in a candlelit dinner on your hotel terrace, savouring exquisite Turkish cuisine beneath the starlit Cappadocian sky.

Day 2: Discovering Cappadocia's Charms

- Morning: Explore the Göreme Open-Air Museum, admiring the ornate rock-cut churches adorned with frescoes.

- Afternoon: Rise above it all with a hot air balloon ride, soaring over the mesmerising landscapes for panoramic views. (Optional: Opt for a sunrise flight for added romance).

- Evening: Wander through Uchisar, taking in the scenic vistas from Uchisar Castle and relishing a romantic dinner with live Turkish music.

Day 3: A Journey Through Time and Love

- Morning: Immerse yourselves in history with a visit to the Derinkuyu Underground City, a marvel of early Christian refuge.

- Afternoon: Hand in hand, hike through the picturesque Ihlara Valley, discovering hidden rock-cut churches amidst canyon walls.

- Evening: Indulge in a Turkish hammam experience for relaxation, followed by a couples' massage.

Day 4: Adventure and Connection

- Morning: Explore Rose Valley on horseback, capturing stunning photos and cherishing scenic trails.

- Afternoon: Enjoy a private picnic in Pigeon Valley, savouring local delicacies together.

- Evening: Witness the sunset over Cappadocia and dine at a cave restaurant with breathtaking views.

Day 5: Beyond the Beaten Path

- Morning: Explore the village of Güzelyurt, immersing yourselves in local culture.

- Afternoon: Hike through Monastery Valley, enjoying cave churches and panoramic vistas.

- Evening: Learn to cook Turkish dishes together in a romantic candlelit setting.

Day 6: Leisure and Pampering

- Daytime: Relax by the hotel pool, indulge in spa treatments, or simply enjoy each other's company.

- Evening: Cherish your final night with a rooftop dinner in Göreme.

Day 7: Departure with Lasting Memories

- Morning: Bid farewell to Cappadocia, carrying cherished memories and a strengthened bond. Enjoy a private transfer to the airport for your departure flight.

Romantic Touches

1. Consider in-room massages or private breakfasts on your balcony.
2. Bring champagne to celebrate special moments.
3. Seek out restaurants with a romantic ambiance.
4. Leave love notes for each other.
5. Capture your love story with professional photos.

Chapter 10: Practical Information and Tips

Currency and Money Matters

P lanning your adventure in Cappadocia goes beyond just flights and lodging; it also involves understanding the local currency and managing your finances effectively. Here's a comprehensive guide to navigating money matters during your trip:

The Currency

Turkey uses the Turkish Lira (TL) as its official currency. As of May 2024, exchange rates fluctuate, but here's an approximate conversion rate to get you started:

1 USD ≈ 18.5 TL

1 EUR ≈ 20.5 TL

Exchanging Currency

1. Airports: Currency exchange booths are available at Kayseri Airport and Nevşehir Kapadokya Airport. Rates may not be the most competitive here, so consider exchanging only a small amount for immediate needs.

2. Banks: Banks offer reliable exchange rates. Look for banks with ATMs displaying international network logos like Visa or Mastercard.

3. Exchange Offices: You'll find numerous exchange offices in major towns like Göreme, Ürgüp, and Avanos. Compare rates before exchanging to ensure the best deal, and inquire about any commission fees.

Travellers Checks

Travellers checks aren't widely accepted. Opt for credit cards or exchanging currency for Turkish Lira for convenience and security.

Credit and Debit Cards

Major cards like Visa and Mastercard are widely accepted, but smaller shops may prefer cash. Inform your bank about your travel plans to avoid issues with card usage abroad, and be mindful of foreign transaction fees.

ATMs

ATMs are plentiful in major towns and cities. Look for those displaying international network logos. Check with your bank about potential withdrawal fees abroad.

Tipping

While not mandatory, tipping is appreciated for good service. In restaurants, a tip of around 5-10% is customary. Leave a small tip for hotel staff or service providers if satisfied.

Costs

Accommodation, food, activities, transportation, and souvenirs all vary in price. Consider purchasing a Cappadocia Pass for discounts on museums and sites, travel during shoulder seasons for lower prices, and utilise public transport and street food to save money. Don't forget to haggle at bazaars for better deals.

By following these tips and planning your budget accordingly, you'll ensure a financially comfortable and enjoyable experience in Cappadocia, collecting cherished memories along the way.

* * *

Transportation Options

To navigate Cappadocia's vast landscapes and charming towns, you'll need to consider various transportation options catering to different budgets and travel styles. Here's a breakdown of your choices.

Within Towns and Villages

1. Walking: Explore central areas like Göreme, Uchisar, and Avanos on foot, perfect for soaking in the local atmosphere and discovering hidden gems at your own pace.

2. Bicycles: Rent a bicycle to venture further afield, allowing for a more active exploration beyond the main tourist spots.

Between Towns and Villages

1. Dolmuş (Minibuses): Economical and popular, dolmuşes operate fixed routes between major towns and villages. Flag one down at designated stops and pay the driver directly upon exit.

2. Taxis: Convenient for longer journeys, taxis offer comfort and flexibility. Negotiate the fare upfront, especially for extended trips.

3. Car Rentals: Renting a car grants ultimate freedom to explore at your own pace, but consider factors like an International Driving Permit, navigation, parking, and driving conditions.

Airport Transfers

1. Airport Shuttles: Many hotels provide shuttle services from Kayseri or Nevşehir airports. Book in advance for convenience.

2. Taxis: Easily available at airports, negotiate the fare beforehand for a direct transfer to your hotel.

Additional Considerations

1. Public Transportation Schedules: Dolmuş frequency may vary, especially outside peak hours.
2. Language Barrier: Basic Turkish phrases or a translation app can assist when using public transportation.
3. Luggage: Dolmuşes may have limited space, so pack accordingly.

Understanding these options ensures a stress-free and enjoyable exploration of Cappadocia, blending comfort, budget, and flexibility seamlessly into your travel itinerary.

* * *

Language and Communication

In Cappadocia, while the stunning scenery and rich history steal the spotlight, communicating effectively can be a concern for some travellers. Here's a detailed guide to navigating the language landscape in Cappadocia and ensuring seamless communication throughout your journey.

Official Language
Turkish is the primary language in Turkey, and Cappadocia is no different. Learning a few basic Turkish phrases will greatly enhance your experience.

English Proficiency

The good news is that English proficiency is on the rise in tourist hubs like Göreme, Uchisar, and Avanos. Many locals working in shops, restaurants, and as tour guides are comfortable with basic English.

Non-Verbal Communication

A smile and friendly gestures can help bridge the language barrier. Turks are renowned for their hospitality, and locals will appreciate your efforts to communicate, even if it's through gestures.

Useful Turkish Phrases

Here are some essential Turkish phrases to help you get started:

- Merhaba (Hello)
- Teşekkür ederim (Thank you)
- Lütfen (Please)
- Evet (Yes)
- Hayır (No)
- Konuşmuyorum Türkçe (I don't speak Turkish)
- Bir şey anlamadım (I don't understand)
- Kaç para? (How much?)
- Para yok (I don't have cash)

Mobile Translation Apps

Downloading a reliable mobile translation app like Google Translate or Microsoft Translator can help bridge communication gaps. These apps can translate spoken language in real-time or translate text using your phone's camera.

Travel Phrasebooks

Consider getting a small Turkish travel phrasebook for quick reference.

These often include essential phrases categorised by situation, making them useful companions during your trip.

Body Language

Understanding basic body language cues in Turkish culture can be beneficial. For instance, a head nod indicates agreement, while a raised eyebrow might signal confusion. A quick internet search on Turkish body language can provide valuable insights.

Embrace the Experience

Don't worry about making mistakes! Turks appreciate efforts to communicate in their language, and any attempt will likely be met with warmth and assistance.

Remember

1. Learn a few basic phrases: This shows respect for the local culture and enhances your experience.
2. Speak slowly and clearly: This makes it easier for others to understand you.
3. Be patient and understanding: Communication might take a bit longer, but with patience and a smile, you'll do just fine.

* * *

Health and Safety Tips

To fully immerse yourself in the enchanting beauty of Cappadocia, it's crucial to plan a safe and healthy trip. Here's a detailed guide to help you create unforgettable memories while prioritising your well-being.

Before Your Trip

1. Vaccinations: Make sure you're up-to-date on routine vaccinations for Turkey and consult your doctor for any additional recommendations.

2. Travel Insurance: Invest in comprehensive travel insurance covering medical emergencies, trip cancellations, and lost luggage.

3. Research Local Health Concerns: Familiarise yourself with potential health risks such as rabies or tick-borne illnesses, and pack necessary supplies like insect repellent.

4. Prescription Medications: Bring an ample supply of prescription medications along with a doctor's note in English.

Staying Healthy During Your Trip

1. Sun Protection: Pack sunscreen, a hat, and sunglasses to shield yourself from the sun's rays, and remember to reapply sunscreen regularly.

2. Hydration: Carry a refillable water bottle and drink plenty of water, avoiding tap water.

3. Food Safety: Opt for bottled water and well-cooked meals at reputable establishments.

4. Personal Hygiene: Practise regular handwashing and carry hand sanitizer.

Safety on the Go

1. Respect Local Customs: Dress modestly and be mindful of cultural norms.

2. Beware of Pickpockets: Keep valuables secure and be cautious in crowded areas.

3. Adventure Activities: Choose reputable companies for adventurous pursuits.

Additional Tips

1. Emergency Numbers: Know important contact numbers like ambulances and police.
2. Learn Basic Turkish Phrases: Showing respect for the local language and culture can enhance your experience.
3. Pack a First-Aid Kit: Include essentials for addressing minor injuries.
4. Be Aware of Surroundings: Stay vigilant, especially in unfamiliar areas.

By following these guidelines and using common sense, you'll ensure a safe and memorable adventure in Cappadocia, allowing you to fully appreciate its breathtaking landscapes and rich culture.

Conclusion

As you turn the final page of this guide, the enchantment of Cappadocia likely lingers in your mind. From the surreal rock formations to the deep-rooted history and lively culture, this extraordinary region promises an unforgettable journey for every traveller.

This guide has provided you with the tools and inspiration to plan your ideal Cappadocian escapade. Whether you crave historical discoveries, thrilling adventures, breathtaking scenery, or cultural immersion, Cappadocia caters to all desires.

Beyond the Guidebook

But remember, this guide is just the starting point. The true essence of Cappadocia lies in the unexpected encounters, the heartfelt connections with locals, and the moments you cherish along the way. Embrace the chance to wander off the beaten path, engage in conversations with welcoming locals, and relish in the simple joys of Turkish hospitality.

Leaving a Mark

As you bid farewell to Cappadocia, take a moment to reflect on the experiences that have touched your soul. Perhaps it's the awe-inspiring sunrise viewed from a hot air balloon, the intricate frescoes adorning ancient cave churches, or the tranquillity of a hidden valley. Carry these memories with you, allowing them to enrich your life and serve as a testament to the magic of Cappadocia.

Returning to the Land of Wonders

Cappadocia has a way of captivating hearts and calling travellers back for more. So, as you say goodbye for now, remember that the door remains open for your return. With its ever-changing landscape, diverse cultural heritage, and undiscovered gems awaiting exploration, Cappadocia guarantees a new adventure with each visit.

We hope this guide has been your trusted companion in uncovering the enchantment of Cappadocia. Now, go forth, explore, make memories, and let Cappadocia cast its spell upon you once again.

Made in the USA
Las Vegas, NV
22 October 2024

10239753R00049